PAUL TROXELL

"Surviving the Shadows"

Living with PTSD from Childhood Trauma

This book was professionally typeset on Reedsy.
Find out more at reedsy.com

"Never give up, Never give in, take what you got and share it with others."

Contents

1

Unveiling the Shadows: A Personal Introduction

The reason I am writing this book is because there are so many people out there struggling and may not know they are suffering from PTDS. There is a stigma that makes it harder for people to be aware of their symptoms and know whether or not they can manage them. Once you grasp the tools needed to combat the triggers that cause some of the intense symptoms of PTSD, you will be able to live more normally. If you don't know what PTSD is, I will break down what the words mean and help you find an approach that works for you.

This book touches home with me because I was diagnosed with PTSD and manic depression disorder. I was ten years old when my life took a turn for the worst, starting on October 6, 1985, after losing my mother to a gunshot wound. Living with PTSD from childhood tragedy was very real to me, and I struggled for years to find healthy ways to heal. My goal is to help you learn what PTSD is, what the symptoms are, the types of PTSD, and the resources you will need to manage your PTSD.

This book is divided into twelve chapters content with a reference chapter, each designed to guide you through understanding PTSD from various perspectives. The chapters will provide you with comprehensive information on the history of PTSD, its symptoms, how it affects the brain, different types of PTSD, and various treatment options available. You will also find personal insights into living with PTSD, which may resonate with your experiences or those of someone you know.

Understanding PTSD is the first step towards managing it effectively. Many people live with PTSD without realizing it, often attributing their symptoms to other causes. By raising awareness about PTSD, I hope to help individuals recognize the signs and seek the help they need. This book is not just for those who have PTSD but also for their families, friends, and caregivers who want to understand and support their loved ones better. I walk you through my own journey with PTSD from my childhood as the result loss of a loved one, while providing helpful technical resources along the way.

2

Beyond the Battlefield: Understanding PTSD

Post-Traumatic Stress Disorder (PTSD) is a mental health condition triggered by experiencing or witnessing a traumatic event. It is characterized by intense, disturbing thoughts and feelings related to the event that persist long after the traumatic experience has ended. Individuals with PTSD may relive the event through flashbacks or nightmares, feel sadness, fear, or anger, and may feel detached or estranged from others.

PTSD can develop in anyone who has experienced a traumatic event, but not everyone who experiences trauma will develop PTSD. The disorder can arise from a variety of traumatic situations, including but not limited to:

- **Combat Exposure**: Military personnel and veterans who have been in combat situations are at high risk.
- **Natural Disasters**: Survivors of events like earthquakes, hurricanes, and floods.
- **Serious Accidents**: Victims of car accidents, plane crashes, and industrial accidents.
- **Violent Personal Assault**: Including physical assault, mugging, and

kidnapping.
- ***Sexual Violence***: Such as rape or childhood sexual abuse.
- ***Terrorist Attacks***: Witnessing or being a victim of terrorism.
- ***Sudden Death of a Loved One***: Especially if the death was unexpected and traumatic. (This was the symptom that diagnosed me with PTSD and manic depression disorder)

Symptoms of PTSD usually appear within three months of the traumatic event but sometimes emerge years afterward. These symptoms cause significant problems in social or work situations and in relationships. They can also interfere with the individual's ability to go about their normal daily tasks.

Understand the types of Childhood Trauma:

Childhood trauma refers to experiences during childhood that are emotionally or psychologically distressing and can have lasting effects on an individual's mental, emotional, and physical well-being. These experiences often occur during critical periods of development and can disrupt a child's sense of safety, security, and trust in others. Childhood trauma can vary in severity and may result from various sources, including:

1. **Abuse:** Physical, sexual, or emotional abuse inflicted by a caregiver, family member, or authority figure.

- Example: Physical abuse, such as hitting, kicking, or burning a child.
- Example: Sexual abuse, including molestation, rape, or exploitation.
- Example: Emotional abuse, such as belittling, humiliation, or

constant criticism.

1. **Neglect:** Failure of caregivers to provide for a child's basic physical, emotional, or psychological needs.

- Example: Physical neglect, such as inadequate food, clothing, or shelter.
- Example: Emotional neglect, including lack of affection, attention, or emotional support.
- Example: Supervisory neglect, where caregivers fail to adequately supervise or protect a child from harm.

1. **Household Dysfunction:** Exposure to dysfunctional family environments, including substance abuse, domestic violence, mental illness, or incarceration of a family member.

- Example: Witnessing domestic violence between parents or caregivers.
- Example: Living with a parent or caregiver who struggles with substance abuse or addiction.
- Example: Having a family member who is incarcerated or involved in criminal activities.

1. **Traumatic Events:** Exposure to traumatic events such as accidents, natural disasters, community violence, or medical procedures.

- Example: Surviving a car accident or other serious injury.
- Example: Experiencing a natural disaster, such as a hurricane, earthquake, or flood.
- Example: Witnessing or being a victim of community violence, such as shootings or gang activity.

1. **Loss or Separation:** Experiencing the death of a loved one, parental divorce or separation, or abandonment by a caregiver. This is the one I will go in depth with, because this impacted me in a very big way, because I lost my mom from a gunshot wound.

- Example: Losing a parent, sibling, or close family member to death.
- Example: Parents divorcing or separating, leading to changes in family dynamics and stability.
- Example: Being abandoned or rejected by a caregiver, leading to feelings of loss and abandonment.

These examples illustrate the diverse range of experiences that can constitute childhood trauma. It's important to recognize that each individual's experience of trauma is unique, and the effects of childhood trauma can vary widely from person to person. Seeking support from trusted individuals, therapists, or support groups can be essential for healing and recovery from childhood trauma.

What is a Trigger?

A trigger is anything that prompts a physiological, emotional, or psychological response in someone, often associated with a past traumatic event. Triggers can be sensory stimuli (like sights, sounds, smells, or textures), situations, thoughts, or emotions that evoke memories or feelings associated with the traumatic event.

There are several types of triggers:

1. **Sensory Triggers**: These can include anything that stimulates the senses, like certain smells, sounds, tastes, textures, or visual cues

that remind the individual of the traumatic event.

2. **Emotional Triggers**: Certain emotions, such as fear, anger, sadness, or stress, can trigger memories or responses related to the trauma.
3. **Cognitive Triggers**: These are thoughts or beliefs that remind the individual of the traumatic event, such as specific words, phrases, or mental images.
4. **Social Triggers**: Interactions with specific people or groups, as well as certain social situations, can act as triggers.
5. **Environmental Triggers**: Places or settings that resemble the location where the traumatic event occurred can trigger memories or emotional responses.

For someone experiencing PTSD symptoms related to childhood trauma, triggers can vary widely depending on the individual's experiences and the nature of the trauma. Triggers might include:

- Seeing someone who resembles the perpetrator of the abuse.
- Hearing a sound or phrase that was present during the traumatic event.
- Smelling a particular scent associated with the trauma.
- Being in a situation that resembles the environment where the trauma occurred.
- Experiencing similar emotions to those felt during the traumatic event.

It's important to note that triggers can be highly individualized, and what triggers one person may not trigger another. Therapy and coping strategies often focus on identifying and managing triggers to help individuals with PTSD better navigate their daily lives.

Navigating Triggers: My Journey Through Childhood Trauma

The Day Everything Changed

I remember the day my world shattered into a million pieces. I was just ten years old when I lost my mother. It wasn't just her physical presence that vanished that day; it was the sense of security, warmth, and love that disappeared with her. Since then, I've been on a journey through the tangled maze of triggers and trauma, learning to navigate a life forever altered by childhood grief.

Triggers are like secret codes that unlock hidden chambers of pain within us. They come in many forms, each one a reminder of the past we're desperately trying to forget. For me, sensory triggers are the most potent. The smell of her perfume, the sound of her laughter, the touch of her hair– they all transport me back to a time when life felt safe and secure. But now, they're just painful reminders of what I've lost.

Emotional triggers are another beast altogether. They lurk in the shadows, waiting to pounce when we least expect it. Fear grips my heart like a vice, reminding me of the uncertainty that lies ahead. Anger simmers beneath the surface, a constant companion fueled by the injustice of her untimely departure.

Cognitive triggers are the stories we tell ourselves, the memories we can't erase. Words that once brought comfort now serve as cruel reminders of a future forever altered. Images flash before my eyes like scenes from a nightmare, leaving me feeling lost and alone.

Social triggers are the hardest to bear. Faces that once brought joy now serve as painful reminders of what I've lost. Places we used to frequent together now feel empty and desolate, their silence echoing the emptiness in my heart.

Environmental triggers shape the world around us, turning familiar spaces into battlegrounds of memory and grief. Sounds that once brought joy now serve as a painful reminder of what's been taken from us.

But a midst the darkness, there is hope. Through therapy and self-reflection, I've learned to confront my triggers head-on, turning them from sources of pain into opportunities for growth and healing. And though the road ahead may be long and winding, I take solace in the knowledge that I am not alone. There are others out there, just like me, walking this path of healing and self-discovery. And together, we'll find our way out of the darkness and into the light.

3

Echoes of the Past: Tracing the History of PTSD

PTSD has been recognized throughout history under various names. Ancient texts describe symptoms resembling PTSD, such as "soldier's heart" in Civil War veterans and "shell shock" in World War I soldiers. In ancient Greece, soldiers who displayed signs of trauma after battle were described in works by Homer and other classical authors. The symptoms were often viewed as a sign of weakness or cowardice.

Evolution of Diagnosis

The formal diagnosis of PTSD was established in 1980 when it was included in the third edition of the Diagnostic and Statistical Manual of Mental Disorders by the American Psychiatric Association. This recognition was significantly influenced by the experiences of Vietnam War veterans, Holocaust survivors, and victims of sexual trauma.

PTSD in Modern Times

The understanding of PTSD has evolved significantly since its inclusion in the DAM-III. Research has expanded our knowledge of the biological and psychological mechanisms underlying PTSD, leading to better treatment approaches. The condition is now widely recognized and accepted as a serious mental health issue that requires appropriate medical and psychological intervention.

In recent years, there has been increasing awareness of PTSD in various populations beyond military personnel, including first responders, victims of natural disasters, and survivors of violent crime. This broader recognition has led to more inclusive research and resources aimed at addressing PTSD in diverse groups.

4

Caught in the Storm: Navigating Common Symptoms

PTSD symptoms are generally grouped into four categories:

Intrusive Memories

- Recurrent, unwanted distressing memories of the traumatic event.
- Flashbacks (reliving the traumatic event as if it were happening again).
- Disturbing dreams or nightmares about the traumatic event.
- Severe emotional distress or physical reactions to reminders of the trauma.

Intrusive memories can be triggered by sounds, smells, or sights that remind the individual of the traumatic event. These triggers can cause a person to feel as if they are reliving the trauma, leading to significant emotional and physical distress.

Avoidance

- Avoiding places, activities, or people that remind one of the traumatic event.
- Avoiding thoughts or feelings related to the traumatic event.

Avoidance behaviors are a way for individuals with PTSD to protect themselves from experiencing distress. This can lead to significant lifestyle changes, such as avoiding certain locations, withdrawing from social interactions, or suppressing emotions related to the trauma.

Negative Changes in Thinking and Mood

- Negative thoughts about oneself or the world.
- Hopelessness about the future.
- Memory problems, including not remembering important aspects of the traumatic event.
- Difficulty maintaining close relationships.
- Feeling detached from family and friends.
- Lack of interest in activities once enjoyed.
- Difficulty experiencing positive emotions.
- Emotional numbness.

These symptoms can lead to feelings of isolation and alienation from others. Individuals may struggle with feelings of worthlessness or guilt, believing that they are somehow responsible for the traumatic event or its aftermath.

Changes in Physical and Emotional Reactions (Arousal Symptoms)

- Being easily startled or frightened.
- Always being on guard for danger.
- Self-destructive behavior (e.g., drinking too much, driving too fast).
- Trouble sleeping.
- Trouble concentrating.
- Irritability, angry outbursts, or aggressive behavior.
- Overwhelming guilt or shame.

Arousal symptoms can make daily life challenging. Constant hyper vigilance can lead to exhaustion and difficulty concentrating. Irritability and anger can strain relationships with family, friends, and colleagues.

Understanding these symptoms is crucial for recognizing PTSD in oneself or others. Early recognition can lead to timely intervention and treatment, improving the chances of recovery.

5

Inside the Mind: How PTSD Rewires the Brain

The Amygdala

The amygdala is the brain's threat detection center. In individuals with PTSD, the amygdala becomes overactive, leading to heightened fear and anxiety responses. This over activity can cause individuals to perceive threats even in safe environments, contributing to hyper vigilance and difficulty feeling safe.

The Hippocampus

The hippocampus is involved in memory formation. In PTSD, the hippocampus often shows reduced volume, which can lead to problems distinguishing between past and present experiences. This reduction can cause difficulties in forming new memories and recalling details of the traumatic event accurately.

The Prefrontal Cortex

The prefrontal cortex is responsible for regulating emotions and executive functions, such as decision-making and impulse control. In individuals with PTSD, the prefrontal cortex may be less active, impairing the ability to control fear and stress responses. This reduced activity can make it difficult for individuals to regulate their emotions and responses to stress.

Neurotransmitter Imbalance

PTSD can cause imbalances in neurotransmitters like serotonin and norepinephrine, which are critical for mood regulation. These imbalances can contribute to symptoms of depression, anxiety, and irritability.

The Brain's Stress Response

When a person experiences a traumatic event, the brain's stress response system becomes activated. This system involves the hypothalamus, pituitary gland, and adrenal glands, collectively known as the HPA axis. In PTSD, the HPA axis may become dysregulated, leading to chronic stress and anxiety. This dysregulation can cause the body to remain in a heightened state of arousal long after the traumatic event has passed.

Impact on Cognitive Functioning

PTSD can also impact cognitive functioning, leading to difficulties with concentration, attention, and memory. Individuals may struggle to focus on tasks, remember important details, or make decisions. These cognitive difficulties can affect daily functioning and quality of life.

Long-Term Effects

Over time, the chronic stress associated with PTSD can lead to physical health problems, such as cardiovascular disease, gastrointestinal issues, and chronic pain. The constant state of arousal can strain the body, leading to long-term health consequences.

Understanding the effects of PTSD on the brain can help in developing effective treatment strategies. By targeting specific areas of the brain and addressing neurotransmitter imbalances, therapeutic interventions can help individuals manage their symptoms and improve their quality of life.

6

Unraveling Complexity between PTSD, Acute Stress Disorder, and Complex PTSD

Acute Stress Disorder (ASD)

Acute Stress Disorder (ASD) occurs in the immediate aftermath of a traumatic event and lasts from three days to one month. Symptoms are similar to those of PTSD but are shorter in duration. They include:

- Intrusive memories or flashbacks.
- Avoidance of reminders of the trauma.
- Negative mood and thoughts.
- Dissociation (feeling detached from oneself or reality).
- Arousal symptoms such as irritability and sleep disturbances.

ASD can be a precursor to PTSD if symptoms persist beyond one month. Early intervention is crucial in preventing the progression from ASD to PTSD.

Post-Traumatic Stress Disorder (PTSD)

PTSD is diagnosed when symptoms persist for more than one month after the traumatic event. The symptoms are more enduring and can cause significant impairment in daily functioning. Unlike ASD, PTSD is often chronic and requires long-term treatment and management.

Complex PTSD (C-PTSD)

Complex PTSD (C-PTSD) results from prolonged or repeated trauma, such as childhood abuse, domestic violence, or captivity. C-PTSD includes the core symptoms of PTSD but also involves additional symptoms, such as:

- ***Emotional Dysregulation***: Intense and unstable emotions, difficulty controlling emotional responses.
- ***Negative Self-Concept***: Deep feelings of worthlessness, guilt, or shame.
- ***Interpersonal Difficulties***: Problems forming and maintaining relationships, often due to trust issues or fear of abandonment.

C-PTSD often requires specialized treatment approaches that address the complex nature of the trauma and its impact on the individual's sense of self and relationships.

Key Differences

- ***Duration***: ASD is short-term (less than one month), whereas PTSD is long-term (more than one month). C-PTSD is associated with prolonged or repeated trauma.
- ***Symptoms***: While ASD and PTSD share similar symptoms, C-PTSD includes additional symptoms related to emotional regulation and self-perception.
- ***Treatment Needs***: ASD may require brief intervention, while PTSD often requires long-term therapy and medication. C-PTSD needs specialized, often trauma-focused, therapeutic approaches.

Recognizing the differences between these disorders is essential for accurate diagnosis and appropriate treatment. Each disorder has unique challenges and requires tailored intervention strategies to support recovery.

7

Roots of the Shadows: Exploring Causes and Risk Factors

What are the Causes of PTSD?

PTSD can develop after experiencing or witnessing a traumatic event. The causes are diverse and can include:

- **Combat and Military Exposure**: Exposure to warfare, combat, and life-threatening situations.
- **Natural Disasters**: Earthquakes, hurricanes, floods, and other catastrophic events.
- **Serious Accidents**: Car crashes, plane crashes, industrial accidents, etc.
- **Violent Personal Assault**: Physical assault, mugging, robbery, or kidnapping.
- **Sexual Assault**: Rape, molestation, and other forms of sexual violence.
- **Terrorist Attacks**: Witnessing or being a victim of acts of terrorism.

Sudden Death of a Loved One: Especially if the death is unexpected or violent, this is where I go in depth and explain in my own journey.

Risk Factors

Not everyone exposed to a traumatic event develops PTSD. Several risk factors can increase the likelihood of developing PTSD:

- *Previous Trauma:* A history of trauma or abuse increases vulnerability.
- *Severity and Duration*: More severe and prolonged trauma is more likely to result in PTSD.
- *Personal History*: A history of mental health conditions, such as anxiety or depression.
- *Lack of Support*: Absence of a strong support system can impede recovery.
- *Gender*: Women are more likely to develop PTSD than men.
- *Occupation*: Certain professions, such as military personnel, first responders, and healthcare workers, have higher exposure to traumatic events.
- *Genetics*: Family history of PTSD or other mental health disorders.

Protective Factors

Conversely, certain factors can protect against developing PTSD:

- **Strong Support System**: Having supportive friends and family can buffer against PTSD.
- **Positive Coping Skills**: Effective coping mechanisms and stress management techniques.
- **Resilience**: Inherent resilience and the ability to adapt to adversity.
- **Access to Resources**: Availability of mental health services and resources.

Understanding the causes and risk factors of PTSD can help in developing preventive measures and identifying individuals at higher risk. Early intervention and support can significantly reduce the likelihood of developing PTSD after a traumatic event.

8

Heart of the Storm: The Personal Impact of PTSD

Emotional Journey

My journey with PTSD began at the age of ten, following the traumatic loss of my mother. The emotional turmoil was overwhelming, and I often felt like I was on an emotional roller coaster. I experienced intense sadness, anger, and confusion, which were difficult to understand and manage as a child. My mother's death left a void in my life that was hard to fill, and I often struggled with feelings of abandonment and guilt.

I remember the day vividly. It was a typical evening, and my mother had been drinking. Her mood started to change, and when I looked at her, her face was full of tears. As a ten-year-old, I was curious why she was crying. At first, I was afraid to ask, but then she said she was leaving and going home. I looked at her with a puzzled look on my face, and she explained that she was going home to see a father that loved her. I questioned if she was okay because of the amount of alcohol she had that night. I remember reassuring her that she was already home and would be fine when she woke up the next morning. As I walked away, she demanded I give her a hug and proceeded to tell me she was leaving me to go home to her father. I remember being sad and going into my bedroom to cry myself to sleep, thinking she was leaving us behind.

The next day, I woke up to my mother lying on the floor with blood all around her with my step-father lying beside her. I quickly dialed 911, and wasn't able to get through, so I panicked and ran across the street for help. The neighbor arrived at the house to call 911. The neighbor waited until someone arrived on scene. My brother and his friend were already awake and in shock of what was going on. I pushed my brother so he wouldn't see the blood on the TV and the floor. My mother was lying in a pool of her own blood. She had died from a gunshot wound to her stomach area. As a child, I was confused and thought she had left us just like she said she would the night before. To this day, I can still remember how sad I felt knowing that my mother wasn't coming back home, and it had me wondering what I could have done to save her from leaving us. My question in my head was why she was gone, and the event in my life set off several triggers that would be hard to manage. I didn't realize that my nightmare of that night would continue to play on in my head triggering a sadness that kept me in constant fear. Losing a loved one, right in front of you with no way I could have saved her.

Physical Journey

Physically, PTSD can manifest in various ways. I began to experience chronic headaches and stomachaches, which doctors initially attributed to stress. Over time, I realized these physical symptoms were my body's response to the trauma I had experienced. I also had trouble sleeping, often waking up multiple times during the night due to nightmares or simply feeling unsafe. The lack of sleep further exacerbated my physical and emotional health, creating a vicious cycle that was hard to break.

PTSD also affected my appetite and energy levels. There were days when I had no appetite and other days when I would eat compulsively, trying to fill the emotional void. The constant stress took a toll on my immune system, making me more susceptible to illnesses. I frequently felt fatigued and lacked the energy to engage in activities I once enjoyed.

This happen over the course of 20+ years, going through really tough times of finding new ways to cope the loss of my mother with managing each trigger that caused major setback emotionally and physically. My PTSD symptoms started right after loss my mother at the age of ten, and after more tragic events in my life into my adult years. The triggers from those events, made it difficult to bounce back. This took me years to finally manage my PTSD symptoms to where I no longer have the major set backs I once had as kid. You never really lose the symptoms, but with the write tools they can be managed.

9

Shadows in Different Shades: Exploring Types of PTSD

Acute PTSD

Acute PTSD refers to symptoms that last for less than three months after exposure to a traumatic event. It is often characterized by:

- **Intense Anxiety**: Feelings of panic or intense anxiety related to the trauma.
- **Hyper vigilance**: Being constantly on alert for potential threats.
- **Intrusive Thoughts**: Frequent and distressing thoughts or memories of the traumatic event.
- **Avoidance**: Avoiding places, people, or activities that remind one of the trauma.

Acute PTSD can be highly disruptive to daily life, making it difficult to concentrate, sleep, or engage in normal activities. Early intervention is crucial to prevent the transition to chronic PTSD.

Chronic PTSD

Chronic PTSD is diagnosed when symptoms persist for more than three months. It often involves:

- **Persistent Symptoms**: Long-term presence of intrusive thoughts, avoidance, and hyper vigilance.
- **Functional Impairment**: Significant impact on daily functioning, including work, relationships, and social activities.
- **Co morbid Conditions**: Higher likelihood of co-occurring mental health conditions, such as depression or substance abuse.

Chronic PTSD can be particularly challenging to manage, as the symptoms are deeply ingrained and may require long-term treatment. Individuals with chronic PTSD may struggle to maintain employment, relationships, and a stable lifestyle.

Complex PTSD

Complex PTSD (C-PTSD) results from prolonged or repeated trauma. It includes the core symptoms of PTSD but also involves additional symptoms, such as:

- **Emotional Dysregulation:** Difficulty managing emotions, leading to intense emotional responses.
- **Negative Self-Concept**: Persistent negative beliefs about oneself, feelings of worthlessness, or deep shame.
- **Interpersonal Difficulties:** Challenges in forming and maintaining

relationships, often due to trust issues or fear of abandonment.

C-PTSD is often associated with severe and chronic trauma, such as childhood abuse or domestic violence. Treatment for C-PTSD typically involves addressing both the symptoms of PTSD and the additional symptoms related to emotional regulation and self-perception.

Secondary PTSD

Secondary PTSD, also known as vicarious trauma, occurs in individuals who are indirectly exposed to trauma through their work, such as healthcare providers, therapists, or first responders. Symptoms include:

- **Emotional Distress**: Feelings of sadness, anxiety, or anger related to the trauma of others.
- **Intrusive Thoughts**: Recurrent thoughts or images of the traumatic events experienced by others.
- **Burnout:** Emotional exhaustion and a sense of being overwhelmed by the trauma of others.

Secondary PTSD can affect those who work closely with trauma survivors and can lead to significant emotional and psychological distress. It is important for individuals in these professions to have access to support and resources to manage secondary PTSD.

Understanding the different types of PTSD can help in developing tailored treatment plans that address the specific needs and symptoms of each individual. Early intervention and appropriate support can significantly improve outcomes for those living with PTSD.

10

From Shadows to Light: Treatment and Management Strategies

Psychotherapy

Psychotherapy, or talk therapy, is a primary treatment for PTSD. Several types of psychotherapy have proven effective, including:

Cognitive Behavioral Therapy (CBT)

CBT helps individuals recognize and change negative thought patterns and behaviors. It includes:

- **Cognitive Processing Therapy** (CPT): Focuses on changing how one thinks about the trauma.
- **Prolonged Exposure Therapy** (PE): Involves gradually confronting trauma-related memories and situations in a controlled manner to

reduce fear and anxiety.

Eye Movement Desensitization and Reprocessing (EMDR)

EMDR involves guided eye movements while recalling traumatic memories, which can help reduce the emotional impact of these memories. EMDR is particularly effective for processing traumatic memories and reducing distress associated with them.

Medications

Medications can help manage symptoms of PTSD. Common medications include:

1. **Sertraline (Zoloft)**: Sertraline is an SSRI commonly prescribed for PTSD. It works by increasing the levels of serotonin in the brain, which can help alleviate symptoms of depression, anxiety, and intrusive thoughts. (Medication I was prescribed in the beginning of my diagnosis)
2. **Paroxetine (Paxil)**: Paroxetine is another SSRI often used to treat PTSD symptoms. Like sertraline, it increases serotonin levels in the brain and can help reduce symptoms such as re-experiencing, avoidance, and hyperarousal. (Medication that was prescribed to me in my adult years.)
3. **Fluoxetine (Prozac)**: Fluoxetine, another SSRI, may also be prescribed to manage PTSD symptoms. It is particularly effective in

treating co-occurring depression and anxiety commonly experienced by individuals with PTSD.

4. **Venlafaxine (Effexor XR)**: Venlafaxine is an SNRI that works by increasing levels of both serotonin and norepinephrine in the brain. It is often used when SSRIs alone are not effective in managing PTSD symptoms.

5. **Duloxetine (Cymbalta)**: Duloxetine is another SNRI that is sometimes prescribed for PTSD. It can help alleviate symptoms of depression, anxiety, and chronic pain often associated with PTSD.

6. **Prazosin**: While not as commonly prescribed as SSRIs or SNRIs, prazosin may be used specifically to reduce nightmares and improve sleep quality in individuals with PTSD. It works by blocking the effects of adrenaline on certain receptors, leading to relaxation of blood vessels and reduced arousal during sleep.

Support Groups

Support groups provide a safe space for individuals with PTSD to share their experiences and receive support from others who understand what they are going through. These groups can be led by a mental health professional or facilitated by peers. Participating in a support group can reduce feelings of isolation and provide valuable coping strategies.

Self-Care Strategies

Self-care is crucial in managing PTSD. Effective self-care strategies include:

- **_Regular Exercise_**: Physical activity can reduce stress and improve mood.
- **_Healthy Diet_**: Eating a balanced diet can support overall well-being.
- **_Adequate Sleep_**: Establishing a regular sleep routine can improve sleep quality.
- **_Mindfulness and Relaxation Techniques_**: Practices such as yoga, meditation, and deep breathing can reduce stress and anxiety.
- **_Hobbies and Activities_**: Engaging in enjoyable activities can provide a sense of accomplishment and joy.

Alternative Therapies

There are some individuals that find relief from PTSD symptoms through alternative therapies, such as:

- **_Acupuncture_**: Can help reduce stress and improve overall well-being.
- **_Art Therapy_**: Allows individuals to express their emotions creatively.
- **_Animal-Assisted Therapy_**: Interaction with animals can provide comfort and reduce anxiety.
- **Music:** can be very therapeutic to calm the anxiety issues that brings you too focus.

Alternative therapies can complement traditional treatments and provide additional support for managing PTSD symptoms.

Developing a Support System

Building a strong support system is essential for individuals with PTSD. This includes:

- *Family and Friends*: Having a supportive network of loved ones who understand and are there for you.
- *Mental Health Professionals*: Regular contact with therapists, counselors, or psychiatrists.
- *Community Resources*: Access to community organizations and resources that provide support and assistance.

A strong support system can provide emotional support, practical assistance, and encouragement throughout the recovery process. The key here, is to find someone that will provide a safety net, that understands you and your symptoms.

Treatment Planning

Treatment for PTSD should be personalized to meet the individual's needs. A comprehensive treatment plan may include a combination of psychotherapy, medications, support groups, self-care strategies, and alternative therapies. Regular follow-ups with healthcare providers are important to monitor progress and adjust the treatment plan as needed.

The idea here is provide check and balances so you set goals to manage your symptoms and your triggers. I would like to add, don't be afraid to ask for help. I learned over the years saying quiet, only makes your symptoms worth. My goal is to have a Facebook Support Group for those struggling with PTSD, so I can provide an extra tool of support.

11

Guiding Light: Resources and Further Reading

Books to Check out:

The Body Keeps the Score by Bessel van der Kolk: This book delves into the intricate ways in which trauma affects the body and brain, offering insights into the healing process and the potential for recovery

Complex PTSD: From Surviving to Thriving by Pete Walker: Pete Walker, a renowned therapist and trauma survivor, explores the concept of Complex PTSD, providing practical strategies for healing and reclaiming one's life.

Waking the Tiger: Healing Trauma by Peter A. Levine: Peter Levine introduces readers to the concept of somatic experiencing, offering gentle yet powerful techniques for releasing trauma and restoring balance to the body and mind Waking *the Tiger: Healing Trauma* by Peter

A. Levine: Peter Levine introduces readers to the concept of somatic experiencing, offering gentle yet powerful techniques for releasing trauma and restoring balance to the body and mind.

Websites

- **National Center for PTSD**: www.ptsd.va.gov This website, hosted by the U.S. Department of Veterans Affairs, provides comprehensive information on PTSD, including resources for individuals, families, and professionals.
- **PTSD Alliance**: www.ptsdalliance.org The PTSD Alliance is a coalition of organizations dedicated to raising awareness about PTSD and providing support to those affected by it. Their website offers valuable resources and information

PTSD.Support Groups

- **PTSD Support Group** on Facebook: Facebook groups can be a valuable source of support and connection for individuals affected by PTSD. This group provides a platform for sharing experiences, seeking advice, and offering support to fellow members. My Facebook Group will be up an running real soon, so reach out to me if you want to join
- **Local support groups through mental health organizations**: Many mental health organizations offer support groups for individuals living with PTSD. These groups provide a safe space for sharing experiences, learning coping strategies, and building connections with others who understand.

.

Hot-Lines

- ***National Suicide Prevention Lifeline***: 1-800-273-TALK (8255) The National Suicide Prevention Lifeline offers free, confidential support to individuals in crisis. Trained counselors are available 24/7 to provide support and assistance.
- ***Crisis Text Line: Text HOME to 741741*** individuals in crisis can connect with a trained crisis counselor via text message, providing support and guidance during difficult times.
- ***Veterans Crisis Line: 1-800-273-8255 and press 1***. This Hot-lines offers support to veterans and their loved ones, providing assistance for issues related to POTSDAM, mental health, and crisis intervention.

Therapy Resources

- Psychology Today: Find a Therapist Tool WWW.psychology to-day.com
- National Alliance on Mental Illness (NAMI): www.nami.org

Had I possessed the resources I'm sharing in my book, I might have grasped my PTSD symptoms far earlier, saving myself years of turmoil. The books and references highlighted in this chapter provide hope and illuminate the path toward healing. I encourage you to revisit this material whenever you require assistance, meticulously exploring any overlooked aspects. I hold a strong conviction that awareness plays a pivotal role in the recovery journey.

12

Embracing the Dawn: A Conclusion of Hope

Living with PTSD from childhood trauma is a challenging journey, but it is possible to manage and overcome its effects with the right support and resources. Understanding PTSD, its symptoms, and how it affects the brain is crucial for developing effective treatment and management strategies. By recognizing the signs of PTSD and seeking appropriate help, individuals can work towards healing and reclaiming their lives.

The journey of living with PTSD is deeply personal and unique to each individual. While the path to recovery may be difficult, it is important to remember that help is available and recovery is possible. Whether through therapy, medication, support groups, or self-care strategies, there are numerous ways to manage PTSD and improve quality of life.

It is my hope that this book has provided valuable insights and practical information to help those affected by PTSD. By raising awareness and understanding of PTSD, we can reduce the stigma associated with this condition and support those on their journey to healing.

Remember, you are not alone in this journey. Reach out for support, utilize available resources, and take steps towards healing. With time, patience, and perseverance, it is possible to live a fulfilling life despite the challenges of PTSD. I will be putting more content out real soon, on how you can start to manage your life again. My purpose is to help people find a new hope for the future, and provide a book that you can come back too, anytime you need to. My book is to inspire people to find the light from their darkness, and give them the tools needed to fulfill their dreams. Remember, you are not alone. I can finally say that I am medication free today, and now able to manage my PTSD symptoms easier, even though I express any method of treatment and recovery you use that will help you to achieve a more healthier and happier you.

13

References

National Center for PTSD. (n.d.). *VA.gov | Veterans Affairs*. https://www.ptsd.va.gov/

Cnc, A. R. (2023, November 9). *How to heal from trauma.* Very well Mind. https://www.verywellmind.com/10-ways-to-heal-from-trauma-5206940

Bonne, O., & Charney, D. S. (2004). Neuropathology of Stress: Prospects and caveats. *Psychiatry*, 67(4), 407–411. https://doi.org/10.1521/psyc.67.4.407.56561

Yehuda, R., & Sarapas, C. (2009). Neuroendocrine aspects of Post-Traumatic Stress Disorder. In *Elsevier eBooks* (pp. 3303–3319). https://doi.org/10.1016/b978-008088783-8.00105-4

Bird, J. (2015). Improving mental well being for survivors of childhood abuse and neglect:
psychological healing and education course in prisons. *Perspectives in Public Health*, 135(1), 21–23. https://doi.org/10.1177/1757913914561701